ESCAPE FROM

THE 73RD FLOOR

ESCAPE FROM
THE 73RD FLOOR

A MEMOIR OF SURVIVING THE
9/11 TERRORIST ATTACK

BRUCE K. WALCH

AND

CAROLIN ARCZYNSKI WALCH

Publisher: Self Published by Bruce and Carolin Walch
Contact: WalchMemoirPR@gmail.com

ISBN: 978-0-578-98014-0
First Edition: September 2021

Disclaimer: Although this publication is designed to
provide accurate information in regard to the subject
matter covered, the publisher and the author assume
no responsibility for errors, inaccuracies, omissions,
or any other inconsistencies herein. The stories in this
book reflect the author's recollection of events. Some
names, locations, and identifying characteristics have
been changed to protect the privacy of those
depicted. Dialogue has been re-created from
memory.

About the cover inset image: Sean Adair was born in NYC in 1959, educated in New Zealand, and worked in photography & video for most of his career. When the morning news of the first plane strike came on TV, Sean rushed up to the roof of his 20th street apartment with his camera, telephoto lens and tripod. It was his wife who alerted him that another plane was approaching, and the series of photos that followed were published around the world. You can see Sean's 9/11 images displayed in a large format at the *9/11 Memorial & Museum* at Ground Zero in NYC. Learn more about Sean at www.adairproductions.com

TABLE OF CONTENTS

Dedication

Author's Note

Prologue

1. The Evening of September 10th

2. Bruce Starts His Day

3. Carolin Starts Her Day

4. Moment of Impact

5. The Descent: 73rd to 3rd Floor

6. The Roar

7. Retreating Back Up & Trapped on the 10th Floor

8. A Clear Stairwell

9. The Lobby

10. She's Coming Down

11. A Wife's Nightmare

12. The Hour after the Collapse

13. Carolin's Missed Call

14. Trying to Get Home

15. On Edge

16. Finally Home

17. Afterwards

About the Authors

Acknowledgments

DEDICATION

This memoir is dedicated to the first responders for their heroic actions to save lives on September 11, 2001.

My deepest gratitude to the group of FDNY firefighters who saved the lives of the small group I was with by showing us a safe path down a stairwell when we were trapped on the 10th floor of 1 World Trade Center (WTC).

Also to Port Authority Police Captain Kathy Mazza, who showed us the way out of the building before it collapsed, and who moments later tragically made the ultimate sacrifice in the line of duty.

AUTHOR'S NOTE

On September 11, 2001, my office was on the 73rd floor of 1 World Trade Center (WTC), also referred to as the "North Tower", the one with the big antenna on it. It was the first tower to be struck by one of the hijacked planes, and the second tower to collapse.

Until now, I have only shared my story with my family and close friends, and with a boy scout troop on one of the anniversaries at the request of a good friend.

I have decided to publish this short memoir now, as we approach the 20th Anniversary of 9/11, in a more formal format, so that it can be shared more easily with family and future generations of my family so that the horrific events of this day, and the heroes and victims that were lost, will never be forgotten.

On September 11th, 2001, like everyday, I commuted by train from New Jersey to the World Trade Center where I work for the Port Authority of NY & NJ as an Environmental Engineer. I took the elevators to my office on the 73rd floor. This is between 7:50 and 8:00 a.m.

At 8:46 a.m., the day took a decided turn for the worse. This is my story.

PROLOGUE

On September 11, 2001, 19 Islamic terrorists hijacked four airplanes to carry out suicide attacks against targets in the United States. In New York City, the twin towers of the World Trade Center (WTC) were targeted by two of the planes. The third plane targeted the Pentagon just outside of Washington, D.C., and the fourth plane never reached its intended target and crashed in a field in Shanksville, Pennsylvania after the passengers stormed the hijackers when they learned what was happening.

At 8:46 a.m., an American Airlines Boeing 767 loaded with 20,000 gallons of jet fuel crashed into 1 WTC, a 110-story skyscraper also referred to as the "North Tower" in New York City. The impact from the plane left a massive, burning hole near the 80th floor. This was the building where I worked on the 73rd floor.

Initially, people thought it was a freak accident. As television news stations broadcasted live video as breaking news, 18 minutes later, at 9:02 a.m., the world watched live as a second Boeing 767, United Airlines Flight 175, appeared and made a sharp turn directly heading toward the World Trade Center. People watched in horror as it made impact into 2 WTC, also referred to as the "South Tower". The plane struck near the 60th floor causing a massive explosion. Burning debris showered onto the streets below. The United States was under attack.

Then, at 9:37 a.m., American Airlines Flight 77 crashed into the Pentagon, the headquarters of the U.S. Department of Defense, in Arlington, VA, just across the river from Washington, D.C. The impact caused an inferno causing part of the giant building to collapse. At their house in Falls Church, VA, 7 miles away, my sister-in-law would feel the blast wave from the impact, shaking the house.

At 9:59 a.m. the world watched in horror when 2 WTC, the South Tower, collapsed in a huge cloud of dust and smoke, spewing smoke down streets as people ran and tried to duck into buildings to escape.

At 10:28 a.m., 1 WTC, the North Tower, collapses. Two of the tallest buildings in New York City, that defined the city skyline and could be seen from miles away, were reduced to a pile of ash and rubble while a large plume of smoke wafted across the river.

The fourth plane, United Flight 93, was hijacked after leaving Newark Airport in New Jersey. Before takeoff, some of the passengers on board learned about the other attacks taking place from people they talked to on their cell phones. They suspected the hijackers planned to crash the plane into another target. Knowing they were going to die, multiple heroic passengers made a secret plan to fight the hijackers. The plane crashed in a field near the town of Shanksville in western Pennsylvania at 10:10 a.m.

The 9/11 terrorist attacks killed 2,977 people from 93 nations: 2,753 people in New York; 184 people at the Pentagon; and 40 people on Flight 93.*

* (Source for Prologue: History.com Editors. "September 11 attacks." History.com September 11 Attacks: Facts, Background & Impact - HISTORY, Updated September 11, 2020.)

1

The Evening of September 10th

The evening of Monday, September 10, 2001 I arrived home from work to our home in Long Branch, NJ around six-thirty, as usual. My wife, Carolin, and I chatted about our day and a dream trip we were planning to take in a few months to Egypt. We talked about a several day small boat cruise on the Nile and seeing the Pyramids. We needed to purchase our plane tickets soon. We also discussed our work plans for the next day. Carolin worked in NJ politics and had an early morning fundraiser to attend in Middlesex County, NJ. We headed up to bed. A cool front was bringing storms later that night. It was supposed to be a gorgeous day on Tuesday.

2

Bruce Starts His Day

The morning of Tuesday, September 11, 2001 my alarm rings at 5:30 a.m., as usual. I hit the snooze button and evaluated the returns of trying to sleep another nine minutes versus just getting up. After struggling with the dilemma for a few minutes I swung my legs out of bed, sigh and get up.

And so my usual morning ritual I have timed to the minute begins: shower, groom and get dressed. I run downstairs, pour a glass of orange juice and guzzle it down, glancing out the kitchen window at the river, marina and some rowers passing by on their morning row.

Meanwhile, Carolin has gotten up because she has an early meeting. Usually I would be out the door before she arose for work. But this morning we kiss goodbye and Carolin takes note of what I was wearing. Later in the day she would scan images on television, trying to catch a glimpse of my orange and blue tie to pick me out from the crowd.

As I drive to the Little Silver train station I cross the Shrewsbury River. I look downstream to the east at the horizon turning orange with the soon to rise sun.

When I arrive in Newark, I hustle out of the train with a crowd, and go through the turnstiles for the PATH train. When the train that will deliver me safely to and directly beneath the World Trade Center pulls up, I hardly have to make an effort to get on the train as the clusters of people around the opening doors squeeze through the doors like a single organism. At the last stop, the World Trade Center, I move out of the train with the crowd, and go up the escalators. I walk up another set of long escalators to the World Trade Center Concourse Level; this is what they called the shopping mall on the lobby level of the WTC; much of it is below the WTC outdoor plaza. I pass the Godiva store, J. Crew, the card shop, The Gap, Banana Republic, The Knowledge Store, America's Coffee, and then spin through the revolving doors to the lobby of One World Trade Center – the North Tower.

I press my ID against the magnetic reader (one of the security upgrades since the 1993 bombing), go through the turnstiles and say hi to the guard; I later heard he died that morning. I take the express elevator to the 44th floor Sky Lobby, switch to a local elevator bank and go up to the 73rd floor, go to my desk, drop my briefcase on the floor, turn on my computer and take in the view. It's between 7:50 and 8:00 a.m.

I'm in the southwest corner of my building. The towers were aligned to the points of the compass. It's an inspiring view to the South, overlooking the confluence of the East River and Hudson River with Battery Park, the Statue of Liberty, Ellis Island and the Verrazano Narrows Bridge as major landmarks looking south. The view either inspires great and brilliant feats of engineering or periods of thoughtful contemplation as one seemingly stares vacantly into the distance. It's a busy port with all kinds of commercial and pleasure craft moving about and commuter ferries plowing back and forth between New Jersey and New York. Big cruise ships often ply the waters and on some occasions, including Fleet Week, a parade of military boats steams by. Two World Trade Center, the South Tower, is just off the southeast corner of my building. On windy days I can feel and hear my building sway and, if I line up the building edge with a window edge,

I can see the movement relative to the South Tower. On overcast days I am often in or above the clouds; sometimes there are even snow flurries on relatively warm days. But on days like this the view is practically limitless. Helicopters and small aircraft routinely fly past the World Trade Center below me, following the Hudson and East Rivers.

I go back down to the 43rd floor to the cafeteria to get a bagel and coffee. Occasionally I would go to the Cantor Fitzgerald cafeteria on the 101st floor, but not today. I return to my office and eat my bagel and drink my coffee and check my e-mail. I respond to some e-mails and send one to a co-worker with a question about permits for a project. Months later when we regained access to e-mail I saw that she replied at 8:44 a.m. Two minutes later a plane would fly into our building. I think about the day ahead, mostly thinking I'd like to get out of work for the day and go biking or kayaking or to the beach or something. I have to go to the bathroom, so I go; I just had coffee after all. It's sometime between 8:40 and 8:45 a.m. The restrooms are located around the central core of the building along with the elevators and stairways. The WTC towers have an open floor plan around the central core that is walled off from the office areas with four sets of doors into the office areas.

At 8:46 a.m. the day took a decided turn for the worse.

3

Carolin Starts Her Day

The morning of September 11th, the political organization I worked for was holding a fundraiser in Edison, NJ. At 8:00 a.m., a small group of party leaders, elected officials and donors gathered to grab a bite of breakfast and chat before starting a busy day. Election season was just getting underway. A little before 9:00 a.m. a few attendees, including a Member of Congress, started getting calls that a plane might have crashed into the World Trade Center.

Since people knew my husband, Bruce, worked at the WTC, someone said "Carolin, I am sure it is nothing, why don't you go into the catering hall manager's office where it is quieter and call Bruce". I called from my cell phone to Bruce's office landline (he didn't own a cell phone yet) but the call wouldn't go through at all. I then tried to call from the catering hall's landline. Each time all I got was a fast busy signal.

The fundraiser was wrapping up so I decided it is best to get to my office and call Bruce from there. There were no TVs where we were at the fundraiser but we did have a small one in the office. I thought we could turn on the news and see what was happening.

I walk outside to my car with my co-worker, Dana Korbman, and we look up at the sky. It is a brilliant deep blue and there is not a cloud in sight. We look at each other and say aloud in unison, "How could a plane accidentally hit the World Trade Center on a day like today?" My cell phone rings and it is my brother John. John lives in Northern Virginia and is a licensed professional engineer who has a lot of experience in construction management for large buildings. He immediately tells me not to worry. He says that it is probably a small plane and a plane like that would basically bounce off of a building like the World Trade Center. I thank him for the reassurance and get in my car to drive the half a mile down the road to my office. I am kind of relaxed at this point because there is no news of anything major. But I'm wondering, why was

Bruce's office phone just a "fast busy" and I didn't even get his voicemail to leave him a message?

4

Moment of Impact

Yes, I was in a bathroom stall when an airplane flew into my building at about 500 miles per hour. Someone later joked that I probably would have relieved myself anyway when the plane hit so it was a good thing I was prepared. I hear an almost imperceptible whoosh, like someone sucking in a gasping breath of air, and then a huge BOOM and I am thrown off my seat into the stall wall to my left and then back the other way while I hear a second, smaller BOOM and then the floor is bouncing like a trampoline as the building sways. Small bits of debris and dust fall from the ceiling and I hear someone slam the door of an adjacent stall and run out of the bathroom. I hear a sound like rushing water. My first thought of what had happened was that I was experiencing an earthquake and I was about 800 feet above the ground.

I quickly finish my business and walk out of the stall to the sinks where I meet a co-worker. The look on his face was unforgettable – one of stupefied, fearful shock with his mouth agape. I apparently reinforced his reaction with a similar look on my face as I exclaimed, "What the hell was that?" At least that's what he told me three weeks later. All I remember is the look on his face.

I make my way back towards the office area through the south doors and meet up with another person I work with. His eyes are wide with fear and he is hustling on his way out.

"What's happening?", I ask.

He replies, "I don't know but something above us exploded and we have to get out. Debris is flying past the windows."

I walk to the southwest corner where my cubicle is. No one is around; everyone else seems to have already left. I look through the south windows and all I see is small debris and paper, lots and lots of paper, some burning, lazily swirling about in the sunshine. I think, something has exploded on another floor and blown out some windows; the building has stopped moving and everything seems stable; I'm not engulfed in smoke and fire; the power is on and no alarms are going off so it's not that bad; there is no immediate urgency here and I do not need to panic. (Granted, I am not completely calm and unconcerned; I do suppress a pang of panic in my gut.) So, I walk to my cubicle, pick up my briefcase – no sense leaving it behind - and notice I had unread e-mail on my computer; I consider checking it for a moment.

Then I see Marco Salcedo, who I work with, checking to see that everyone was out of the area. He was one of the floor fire wardens (they make sure people do the right things during fire drills which means walk out to the central core area and stand around. They also are responsible for checking the floor to make sure everyone has left in the event of a real emergency). He has a flashlight. He says "Come on. Let's go. Everyone's gone." We proceed to the central core area where the stairwells are located. By then the area was filling with smoke and dust coming through the ceiling and the elevator shafts. Smoke and dust were pouring out of the elevator shafts and something – fuel and water, I learned later – was rushing down the shafts as well, spilling into the elevator lobby.

A maintenance worker was closing the fire doors in the corridor just beyond the elevator bank and seemed ready to lock them when he saw us and waved us through the doors and said, with some urgency, "Come ON". These doors are closed as a fire and smoke barrier during fire emergencies. We opened a stairwell door and entered – I think it was Stairwell B. I don't know why we chose this stairwell. There were three to choose from. Some stairwells go all the way down and some you have to transfer through hallways before you can continue up or down. But in we went.

5

The Descent: 73rd to 3rd Floor

The stairwell is packed with people. Two lines of people are marching down so we merge into a line and start down. It is excruciatingly slow going; everyone in the building that can escape is trying to get down the stairs. But it is a very orderly descent. I mean, no one is thinking the building might collapse. All the trouble is supposedly above us. People are scared and some are hyperventilating and some are panicked and have to be carried, but nobody is out of control or shoving their way past others. People are helping those that need it.

One guy I know, John Azzaro, takes off his shirt and rips it up for people to put over their mouths; some smoke and dust was building up in the stairwell but it was not too bad. He was talking a lot and trying to give everyone a piece of his shirt.

An older man advised, "Calm down. We don't need to get worked up here. We're going to get out. You're making people nervous. Everything's going to be fine." I think the man was trying to convince himself.

John replied, "I know. That's just me. I talk a lot. I'm fine."

Paul Pietrapaolo, another co-worker, was helping one woman who could not walk because she was so panicked. He stopped on a landing and as I passed him I asked if he needed some help. He said, "That would be nice." I paused but two other men stopped to help carry her down and I turned and continued down. Another woman was panicked and hyperventilating and I tried to assure her that everything was going to be fine; we just had to walk down the stairs; all the trouble was above us.

When we got to around the 60th floor, the injured and burned started coming down from the 78th floor and above. I remember one woman in particular walking down the stairs in a mumbling state of shock with her arms outstretched like that Vietnamese girl in the photograph after she had been burned by napalm.

Skin hung from her arms and her hair was singed into a lopsided lumpy mat. Her clothes were not so much burned off of her as they were burned into her. Her face was so burned that those who knew her probably would not have immediately recognized her. Someone was walking down with her but he could not reach out to help her or comfort her because of her burns. All he could do was talk her down and encourage her.

Around that time we met the first of the firefighters on their way up. They must have taken the elevators up to the 44th floor or they never would have made it this far. They were young guys with the strength and stamina to move up the stairs quickly. They were asking where we had come from and what the conditions were on those floors. Someone told them it was pretty bad on 80. Later, when we were on the street, we met up with people who worked on the 80th floor. They almost could not get off their floor because the impact had jammed all the doors into their frames. Marco, whom I left the 73rd floor with, and I told the firefighters that 73 was getting pretty smoky when we had left but there was no fire.

In all, on my way down, I saw maybe 50 firefighters going up. Many more were stopped on other floors, gasping for breath, evaluating the situation on those floors and making fateful decisions. Many of them were young guys lugging hoses, oxygen tanks and other equipment that must have weighed 100 pounds. Other not so young men were also huffing their way up.

At one point one of the older guys, a superior officer I presume, asks someone to help a firefighter who is stopped next to me gasping for breath. He wants someone to lug his hose up one flight of stairs. I step forward to help, but another, younger guy takes the hose. I turned and continued down.

Then Marco and I meet another co-worker of ours going *up* the stairs. He told us he had already been down to the 44th floor and turned around.

We both ask, "What the hell are you doing?"

He says, "I have to get my briefcase. My house keys and wallet and everything are in it."

"You're an idiot if you go up. Our floor was already filling up with smoke when we left."

"But how will I get home or into my house?" he asks. "My wallet and keys are up there."

"You'll get home somehow. But if you go back up, you're being stupid and taking an unnecessary risk. You can get your things later."

We thought we had convinced him to turn around but later in the week I learned he was listed as missing. He did make it out, though. After he got out he went home and shut himself in and did not answer the phone for several days until he got a message from the Chief Engineer at the Port Authority expressing his regret for the family's loss and that counseling was available for family members.

While we were descending, someone (a guy I recognized from my train, but did not know) who had internet on his cell phone began getting news of what had happened. The news started to spread that a plane had hit our building. I immediately thought of the small planes that flew past the World Trade Center regularly. But a hit by one of those would hardly be noticed away from the immediate area of impact. I remember remarking, "You know, the World Trade Center is a pretty easy landmark to avoid, especially on a perfectly clear day. A plane just does not hit the World Trade Center on a beautiful, clear day by accident." Then I think the guy said that two planes had hit – one in the other tower – and they were big planes – 767s. I do not remember specifically when I became aware of the second plane. We had neither heard nor felt the second plane hit the other tower.

We got down to the Sky Lobby on the 44th floor and exited the staircase we were in. For some reason we were redirected out of the stairwell we were in or we came to one of those transfer hallways and we just took the door out. The Sky Lobbies are located on the 44th and 78th floors at the transition between different elevator zones. These are also transfer points for stairwells. Looking at the buildings from a distance, they were the two bands one-third and two-thirds of the way up that looked a little different from the rest of the main facade. We headed toward one staircase on the north side but there was a large group of people waiting to get down that staircase or onto an elevator. Smoke was filling the floor from the south side and only emergency lighting was on. I glanced out the windows and the view seemed fairly normal except it seemed a bit gray for such a bright day. I said, "This is not good. We're going to be stuck here. Or people will keep coming down and the smoke will get worse and people will panic."

Someone agreed with me saying, "The hell with this." So the group I was with turned around and continued down the staircase we had just come out of.

Up to this point, the air has been fairly clear; there was some smoke and dust but nothing too bad except in the Sky Lobby; the smoke there must have been from the fireball and smoke traveling down the elevator and mechanical shafts. The power had been on and not many alarms had sounded. Now as we started down from the 44th floor, conditions began to worsen. The smoke and dust got a little worse; alarms were sounding; power flickered on and off; water began cascading down the stairs bringing with it a faint odor of diesel – jet fuel – and making the footing slippery. Things began to get more confused as we descended and firefighters directed us to different staircases, making way for them and their equipment to go up the stairs.

The firefighters were everywhere now, doing floor searches, continuing higher or collapsing for a moment's rest before continuing. Vending machines were broken into and drinks passed around; some of us expressed that the drinks should be left for the firefighters and that became the general consensus. Some floors or ceilings had partially collapsed and there were small fires and live electrical wires sputtering and sparking across the floor and in the air. During this time, I saw one man, Anthony Infante, with Port Authority Public Safety, several times. He was trying to get a handle on the scope of the disaster, asking people questions about the conditions on the upper floors. I remember seeing him on some higher floors as well. He seemed to be everywhere. He died saving others.

I finally got down as far as a stair landing with the stairs in front of me leading to a door to the mezzanine in the building's lobby. People right in front of me were exiting the stairwell through the door. Once I got through those doors and made it to the mezzanine I could find an exit out of the building. By this time alarms were sounding, emergency strobes were flashing, electricity was flickering on and off and water was pouring down the staircase. But I felt okay, if somewhat anxious. I was about to get out of the building. I would be safe once I got out. I was seconds from the door. Maybe ten steps away.

Then everyone stopped in their tracks and looked around. Something was happening.

6

The Roar

I heard what sounded like a waterfall and the volume
began to build. The sound built into a rumbling roar
that I could sense was coming from above me as I felt
the building begin to shake and vibrate. I started
ducking and looking up, as did everyone else,
wondering what the hell was coming down the stairs.
The power went out and emergency lights flashed on.
The roar grew louder and louder and the rumble grew
deeper and deeper, shaking the building. It was like a
hundred locomotives coming at me. The emergency
lights went out and it was pitch black. Were the
elevators plummeting to the ground? Was something
coming down the stairs? Did another airplane hit the
building? Was something collapsing?

Then there was what seemed like a final, deep, resounding thud. Debris and dust and smoke poured into the stairway from the door I had almost reached. People below me turned from the door and started screaming, "Go back up! Get back up!" Someone screamed, "The first floor collapsed! It collapsed!" We didn't know it at the time but we had just missed possibly being crushed by the other tower's collapse. Apparently the area of the mezzanine we were about to walk out onto collapsed from the impact and weight of debris and that's what the person screaming about the collapse had seen. We stumbled back up the stairs choking on the dust and smoke. People kept yelling "Go back up! Go back up!" And someone was yelling "Go back up to where? Go back up to where?" We kept going, opening doors and trying to get onto another floor where we could see and where the air was clear enough to breathe but every door we opened led to more darkness, smoke and dust. Behind all this confusion there was an eerie, wailing, whistling, beeping sound which I found out about later. For the first time a rush of fear coursed through my body. I thought there was actually a chance I might not make it out. I might get seriously hurt. I might die.

7

Retreating Back Up
&
Trapped on the 10th Floor

We finally made it onto the 10th floor where there was some light from windows and the air was breathable. We tried other sets of stairs but there were fires and they were smoke-filled or blocked. We made our way into an exterior office space to regroup. Now there were only about twenty of us and five or so firefighters. I don't know what happened to everyone else. I remembered a stairway full of people and now there were only about twenty.

We seemed to be safe; we could see and breathe; everything was quiet, very quiet; everything seemed quite calm, considering what was happening. I remember thinking that, if the first floor had in fact collapsed, we could always get down to the second floor and jump – no big deal. I knew we couldn't jump from where we were now.

There were telephones. I picked one up and got a dial tone. I called Carolin at her office. I figured this had hit the news by now and she might be getting a little worried. I knew I was OK but she didn't. It was about 10:15 a.m. but I had no real concept of the time that had passed - an hour and a half since the plane slammed into my building - or just how bad it was outside of the office I was in right now. I didn't realize that most of the world was watching, not believing what they were seeing. I thought I might be telling her about something she hadn't heard about yet.

Adam Neary, he worked for Carolin, answered. I said, "Get Carolin on the phone. It's Bruce."

He said something like, "What? Oh my God! It's you!" and yelled to Carolin.

Carolin picked up the phone and started saying, "Bruce, I love you I love you I love you. Where are you?" I told her I was still in the building but I was OK. She said, "You have to get out of there! Part of your building fell off! Get out!" She was panicked. Between phone calls from friends, family and people she worked with she had been catching glimpses of coverage on a TV with poor reception in her office. What she had seen was not part of my building falling off but was the other tower's collapse, but she did not know that yet.

I said, "Yeah, I just heard something loud. I guess that was it. I'm on the 10th floor and I'm OK. We seem to be safe here."

"Do you realize what's happening?" she asks.

"Yeah, a plane hit my building." I thought it was a strange question. After all, I was in the middle of it. "How bad does it look?"

She replies, her voice rising, "Yeah, a plane hit your building. Planes hit both buildings and a plane hit the Pentagon and a bomb went off at the State Department and there are more planes out there. I'm just trying to give you the scope of what's happening so you understand. There might be another plane headed for New York! You have to get out of there!" I paused for a moment. I wasn't sure what to make of what she was telling me or that I needed to hear everything she was telling me. I didn't feel quite as calm anymore.

"Well, we seem to be safe here but we can't get out right now." The firefighters were talking something over and I thought I needed to get ready to do something. So I said, "I have to go." Apparently I sounded pretty calm and I did still feel pretty calm despite a quietly suppressed panic. Later, Carolin expressed her incredulity at my contention that "we seem to be safe here." We said I love you a bunch of times and I said I'd be OK but I have to go and I hung up. Several minutes later, Carolin watched my building collapse.

The firefighters seemed frustrated; one looked supremely pissed off at what was happening and broke some windows out for air. It seemed like they were considering getting us out through the windows somehow. I walked over to the windows and glanced out and it was like dusk and everything was covered in dust and it was smokey and gray. The last I had seen it was a beautiful sunny day. I was looking out towards West Street, towards the World Financial Center and New Jersey. To the south I saw what looked like a fire truck and an ambulance, but they were covered in dust or debris, their lights still flashing. That was strange enough but something else was amiss. Then I realized that I didn't see any people – not a single person. I thought I would have seen firefighters and police and emergency vehicles and media people all over the place with onlookers in the background behind hastily erected barriers. I started looking around more and vaguely remember seeing shapes that didn't make sense. Then I think something in my mind triggered and I made a subconscious decision that I did not need to see what I was looking at right now. I looked down at the floor and shrunk away from the windows.

I turned and saw an older man who I had seen before and who works with the Port Authority. He had been very shaky and was breathing hard. I was concerned he might have a heart attack. I got him a chair and asked if he wanted to sit by the broken windows where there was more air. He waved me off and shook his head no, saying he was all right.

We were all just standing around. The smell of concrete dust, smoke and burnt plastic permeated the air. When I returned to the site a month later, and on subsequent trips, the smell in the air would stir up vivid memories of this day.

Then some more firefighters came into where we were and said something about having to get out or there was a way out. One firefighter was on the radio; I overheard him say to get the civilians out and then they, the firefighters, were evacuating. That didn't sound too good to me – the fact that firefighters were evacuating, too. He said, "All right everyone. We're going to get you all out of here. Does anyone have flashlights?" Marco had one and there were maybe a couple more. Again the firefighter said, "OK, we're leaving. Anyone with flashlights try to show the way for others. Anything you don't need, leave it here." I picked up my briefcase, which I had somehow held onto. I figured I could drop it on the way if I had to.

We started lining up to leave and I held back to make sure people that seemed less steady made it ahead of me, including the older man I mentioned before. I pulled up the rear and was the last civilian off the floor. One firefighter smiled at me as I passed and patted my shoulder. We walked down the hall and started down the stairs. Now it was dark and smoky with water pouring down the stairs. On the sixth floor we had to move out of our stairwell because it was blocked by fire, debris, or something else. We waded through a locker room knee-deep in water where ceiling tiles and equipment were hanging from the ceiling and on the floor; it was hard to see what it was. I saw a Port Authority policeman with a dust mask on. He looked scared. It seemed that all the stairwells were impassable.

A young fireman was leading the way and he stopped and said he didn't know a way out. Marco, who knew the building fairly well because of his work, said, "No. Keep going. I know there's a door around the corner."

We walked up to the door just as a firefighter burst through the door and said, "You can go down here. It's clear."

8

A Clear Stairwell

We started down the stairwell. Flashlights flashed back
and forth and emergency strobes were flashing and the
eerie, wailing, whistling, beeping sound started up
again. It was all confusing and hallucinatory. The sound
was coming from a small bit of equipment on the
firefighters that I think also lit up. They kept turning
them off. They didn't look too happy. I thought they
were wearing personal air monitors that were going off
because of smoke, carbon monoxide, explosive
atmosphere, whatever was in the air. I also started to
wonder for the first time what might have been in the
airplanes – chemicals or biological agents of some
kind? I found out later that these sounds were distress
signals from their brother firemen in the other tower's
collapse or from the upper floors of my building. I

heard that some floors in my building may have collapsed before the whole building came down. It must have been getting very bad up there.

I came up from behind to the older gentleman again. He had a handkerchief over his face and was going very slowly and shakily. I had a handkerchief too and I dipped it in the water that was now rushing down the stairwell to help block the smoke more but it came back to my face reeking of jet fuel. I slowed to walk beside him and asked if he was OK or if he wanted help getting down. Again he waved me off, saying he was all right. I walked with him for a moment and thought about walking down with him to keep him company and make sure he got down. Then I thought I should probably just go ahead and get out as fast as I could; we're almost down and we'll all be fine. I did experience survivor's guilt later and this man was one of the particular triggers for it, until I saw pictures of him outside the collapse and then I saw him at work.

9

The Lobby

I finally got down to the lobby level. I remember having to duck out of the stairwell, for some reason, and stepping over something. I paused.

The arms of the turnstiles were all down. Everything was dust and smoke and gray. In front of me and to the left, six or so firefighters and police were lined up with their arms outstretched pointing to my right. They were covered in dust and looked like ghosts. Behind them to my left it was dark and smoky with only vague shapes and some fire visible. There was no one else there. I went through the turnstiles and started to my right towards the doors and wall of windows, only they weren't there; they had all been blown out. Another ghostly figure, a Port Authority police officer, was at the windows and she told us to hold something over our heads, and move close along the building towards West Street and the World Financial Center and then run and don't stop. Marco remembers her. Her name is Kathy Mazza. Her ghostly appearance and that of the others in that lobby were prophetic of their fate.

Earlier in the evacuation there had been a bottleneck of people at the doors to exit the building. Officer Mazza used her firearm to shoot out the floor-to-ceiling glass in the lobby. Her action allowed hundreds more people to escape quickly, saving lives. She was killed from the collapse of my building soon after she directed us out.

10
She's Coming Down

I had to look up. I saw my building on fire on one side
and a huge, gaping, black hole on the adjacent side. The
top was engulfed in smoke and flames. It was surreal.
The building did not look so big and tall with the
gaping hole and the raging fire. The flames shooting
out of the building were almost cartoonish, they were
so big. I thought there was no way anyone could fight
that fire and that the poor people above it were going
to go through hell; I couldn't imagine the scene up
there. The fact that it was all happening about 50 yards
above my head when I was looking out of the 73rd
Floor window not quite an hour and 45 minutes earlier
shook me. Something else bothered me but I did not

know what. Something, besides the obvious devastation I was looking at, did not seem right; something was out of place. In fact, something was not there. It did not register in my head, because it was not fathomable, that the other tower was not there.

I looked back down and started running again, glancing up over my shoulder occasionally at the building, both to see it and to check if anything was going to fall on me. Everything was covered in debris and gray dust. I was stepping over things but I didn't know what they were. From what I heard later, that particular area I was running through was where people had crashed after having fallen or jumped from the building.

At first I held my briefcase over my head (yes, I still had it) but then I realized that whatever fell from the building was not going to be stopped by a soft, leather briefcase. A woman who was with us had her heels off and was gingerly stepping through the debris. We told her she needed to move faster and not worry about her feet. We ran across West Street and then started to walk north, going under the pedestrian bridge between 1 WTC and the World Financial Center. I paused to pose a question, "Which way should we go? Head for the river? South to Battery

Park? North?" The consensus was to go north. We continued north and walked about a block. Again I could not understand the absence of any people except the few of us running from the building. I don't remember anyone else coming out of the building behind us, either.

I turned to look up at the tower again. As I looked, the windows of the upper floors blew out and debris spewed from the building in what seemed like a massive explosion. Then I saw the antenna begin to teeter from side to side and start to sink. Then the upper floors started collapsing. They pancaked down, one on top of the other. I was stunned and watched it until I noticed firemen and police running away. One firefighter ran past me yelling "Get the hell out of here! She's coming down!" So I turned and ran. The same roaring and rumbling noise I heard in the stairwell was building again. I looked back and saw the tower collapsing and the huge cloud of debris and dust racing toward me. Marco, who was just ahead of me, and I ran until it appeared that the dust cloud was going to catch us. I assumed the cloud could kill us by asphyxiation as easily as the building falling on us. Then I thought that the steel and concrete from the building was going to crash through the streets and rip open gas and steam lines causing explosions and fire all over the area.

We ran around a building corner to try to avoid the dust cloud and crossed the street where someone was holding a door open and waving us in. We ran in and pulled the door shut behind us as the cloud enveloped the building. It turns out we had run into the Stuyvesant High School on Vesey and West Streets. The students were about to evacuate and the lobby was crammed with students and teachers. I wondered why they were still there. I was nervous about a stampede and moved to the side of the lobby; smoke was leaking into the building. The students were asking who we were and what all the smoke and dust was from. We told them part of the WTC had collapsed – because that's all I thought had happened – the upper floors of my building. One of the students informed me I had the pleasure of escaping to the best high school in the country. What a bonus. Finally, we all walked out the other side of the building, another block away, and continued walking north.

Lined up in formation on West Street were firefighters with grim expressions on their faces, nervously shifting about. I thought they looked just like soldiers about to enter battle, knowing, or more likely not knowing, what lay ahead of them.

11

A Wife's Nightmare

After speaking to Bruce when he was on the 10th floor, I returned to the conference room where my co-workers and the TV were. The angle of the camera on the news broadcast I had watched before he called looked like one whole side of his building had fallen off. We then learned it was actually 2 WTC, the South Tower, collapsing. The entire building collapsed. How was this possible? We were in shock and speechless.

I then made short calls to family to let them know Bruce had just called, that he was on the 10th floor, and that he seemed to be safe, but "couldn't get out right now."

We then watched in horror as Bruce's building collapsed. The whole building, all 110 floors of it, pancaked into a big pile of debris and dust. Just a few minutes earlier he had told me he was on the 10th floor and he seemed to be safe but didn't think he could get out. My mind was racing and I was panicking. I cried and got down on my knees and prayed. Our family and friends were calling me. Some were offering words of hope, while some started to offer condolences. My co-workers, Dana and Adam, were trying to assuage my worst fear. I think I was in a state of shock, subconsciously coming to some kind of slow understanding that my husband was dead. My soulmate and all of our future dreams were evaporating in moments.

The time grew longer with no word from Bruce.

12

The Hour after the Collapse

Then I knew I had to call Carolin; she certainly thought I was dead. I tried someone's cell phone but it didn't work. Pay phones had lines at them and they generally weren't working anyway. Police, government, unmarked and emergency vehicles were racing into and out of what became known as Ground Zero. I thought I stood a good chance of getting hit by one of them as I crossed the street. How absurd that would have been? After escaping from the World Trade Center, getting killed by an emergency response vehicle.

I ducked into one building, a small auto parts store, to try to find a phone and saw one of my co-workers from the floor above me, Paul Johnke. I didn't recognize him at first because he was covered in dust, absolutely caked with the stuff. He said, "Bruce!" and seemed shocked to see me. And then I recognized him. He was shaking slightly as he tried to wipe the dust out of his eyes. He described, his voice also shaking, how he had been in the lobby of our building helping people out when the first tower collapsed and he was plunged into dust and darkness, unable to see or breathe. "The only thing I could think about was my kids," he said.

I said, "We gotta get out of here" and he said, "Get out of here to where? The whole place is shut down. Nothing's coming in or out of the city." I asked him if he was OK as he plopped down in a chair, shaking. He said that he was and I told him I was going to head north and Marco and I left. The guy running the store was on his phone and it looked like he was going to be on it for a while.

It wasn't until an hour later that I found a phone that worked. I tried someone's cell phone and the call went through to Carolin's office. Adam answered and I think he almost shit in his pants when I said, "Adam, it's Bruce. Put Carolin on." He said she wasn't there. She hadn't known what to do; people had started calling her and expressing condolences. One of her brothers, Dan, had called and said, "Carolin, I'm so sorry." He later told us that as he watched the first building collapse he thought to himself, "OK. There's still a fifty percent chance he's still alive." When my building collapsed he thought, "OK. Now there's a zero percent chance he's alive and that only a miracle can save Bruce." Others said they just knew I was OK. So Carolin had gone out to get cigarettes.

Adam advised me, "Just head north. Go to Central Park. More airplanes may be out there." Feeling comforted by the fact that more airplanes might be on their way and that I could not talk to Carolin yet, I continued north with Marco.

13

Carolin's Missed Call

I returned from the convenience store a few minutes later with a soda and cigarettes. I had kicked the terrible habit 6 months earlier but this situation was just too much. Adam came running out of the office to greet me, "Carolin, Bruce called, he is alive! He made it out of the building before it collapsed!" I was elated but it was hard to believe. I wanted to believe Adam but I just couldn't get to a state of calm since I hadn't talked to Bruce myself. I think I was still in shock and subconsciously had created a wall to protect these extreme emotions being created by this traumatic situation. I needed to talk to Bruce myself for proof he was alive. And if he was alive, I didn't know how he was doing, what he was doing, or how he would get

51

home. The fear of additional attacks in New York also caused a nagging anxiety.

I didn't know what to do so I decided it was best to stay in my office. I would wait until I heard from him again, and to hear his voice myself.

14

Trying to Get Home

It was surreal walking through the city. It seemed everyone was outside; many walking north, trying to make phone calls, clustered around radios or TVs or just clustered together in groups talking, all with similar expressions of disbelief on their faces. Everyone seemed to be gravitating to each other. We finally got to 34th Street and 7th Avenue. Penn Station was to the right so we started that way even though we knew we weren't getting out of the city anytime soon. Then I noticed many people were walking the opposite way. I asked someone if there was a ferry that way. He said he wasn't sure. I decided to give it a try since I knew the trains were not running. Marco and I shook hands and again marveled at our good fortune to be alive. We said if we couldn't get out of the city we would meet up at this corner again and we parted ways.

As I crossed the street a man walked out of a bar, I believe it had an Irish name, holding an American flag over his head. "Keep your heads up, people", he admonished. "They can't do this to us and keep us down. Stand proud!"

I got down to the water and there was a long, snaking line for the ferry. I asked where it went and someone said Weehawkin. The ferry to Hoboken wasn't running. I thought, "Well, at least it's the right side of the river" and got in line. The sun was intense and I remembered I had my umbrella in my briefcase. I popped it open and tried to share the shade with those near me as we snaked through the line. As we talked, I said I had been in the WTC and I began getting the disbelief and astonishment that I was still alive. People were almost reverent, it seemed. Someone said I was so lucky I should play the lottery. By the time I got to the front of the line they were running ferries to Hoboken which was much closer to where I wanted to be.

On the ferry I run into someone I recognize from work; he was in the Engineering Department, too. We exchange a few words about what had happened to us.

The main thing we said and felt was how good it was to see someone else we knew who had survived. This feeling became a recurring theme whenever I saw someone else I worked with or just knew by sight; how good it was to see someone else who had survived. I had become convinced by this time that many people I knew were dead. It was whisker-close for me and I had passed people on the way down the stairs. But it turns out, because of the diversions I encountered, my route out was longer and more tortuous than what was experienced by a lot of people I know.

The ferry was working its way south along the Hudson as it made a long diagonal across the river towards Hoboken. This is when I really first noticed the fighter planes patrolling the skies over New York. I had heard the noise from them before but this was the first time I looked up and saw them streaking across the sky. Then I looked around the river and saw the many Coast Guard boats patrolling the waters. While the sight of our military in action was reassuring it was also disconcerting to know they were there to protect us from more attacks.

As we neared lower Manhattan, what conversation there had been hushed to silence. Everyone stared at where the World Trade Center had stood. It was as if no one could speak and have anything worth saying that would add anything to the mere act of witnessing what we saw. A huge cloud of dust and smoke obscured much of lower Manhattan and streamed south and east as it was blown by the wind. Although by this time I knew they were gone, I kept searching for the outlines of the towers to emerge from the smoke.

When the ferry arrived at Hoboken, emergency personnel directed any of us who had been in the downtown area towards a decontamination area they had set up. At first they were spraying people with fire hoses but then they set up showers and ran people through those. I thought of skipping it and just continuing on my way home, but still I wondered what else might have been in the planes and on me other than a little dust and asbestos, so I went through the showers. I hardly got wet so the decontamination was totally ineffective. But after the showers, people were taking down names, addresses and where you had been that day, so at least I was logged into the system if it turned out there was a more serious concern.

15

On Edge

I get into the station and call Carolin from a pay phone.
This is the first time we talk after she thought I was
dead. After telling each other "I love you", she asks,
"Where are you? Can you get anywhere? Should I
come pick you up?" I tell her to definitely not try to
come get me and that I would find a way home and
meet her there. I went out to the tracks and the train I
needed to get home was sitting there but they had
closed the gates and I couldn't get on. The train pulls
away so I go check the schedule to see what other
trains I could catch to at least get to Newark. There
aren't any so I walk out of the station to see if there are
any buses to catch.

I get outside and look around; I'm on edge and wary of everything. Suddenly there is a commotion and a man runs from the emergency workers, with them running after him telling him to stop. Does this guy have a gun or a bomb? Then someone yells, "It's coming in!" and people scatter, running in all different directions. People are running down the train tracks. I hear a droning sound and look up and around wondering what is coming in and why would they attack Hoboken? I even start to duck. Nothing happens and the panic eventually subsides. I start walking towards some buses and where people are standing around apparently waiting for buses. I ask around and eventually just wait at a spot where a group is waiting. A bus comes that is headed to Journal Square, another major transportation hub in Jersey City. I figure I can get to Newark somehow from there and I take the bus. At Journal Square I discover the PATH train is not running, which was no great surprise since it connects to the World Trade Center under the Hudson River, and I wander about until I find a private bus charging $5 to get to Newark. I pay the money and hunker down in a seat.

As we travel to Newark I see many people walking over highways and bridges. Obviously the transportation system is completely screwed up and I feel lucky to have found this bus. At the Newark train station we can't get off the bus. A policeman tells the driver not to let anyone off because we have to go through decontamination or something. Passengers start to get extremely irate and animated and finally the driver realizes he had better open the door or his bus is going to be ripped apart. As I walk away from the bus I hear the cop tell the driver that he's out of business for the day and directs him to park the bus.

In the train station I check the schedules and find my train home. It's actually not too far off from when I would normally catch the train on my regular commute. I have a bit of time and notice I'm starving; I'd only had a bagel this morning. I get a hot dog and start wolfing it down. A man approaches me and strikes up a conversation. He notes that I look a little ragged and I tell him I was in the WTC when it was attacked. He is taken aback for a minute and says, "Boy, you've had a rough day." But then he says, "Listen, I normally wouldn't ask, but I was wondering if you could help me out. I'm trying to get…" and I cut him off, recognizing the spiel of someone trying to get some cash; he's not someone in dire need but a con man.

I almost lunge at him but then I just spew at him, cussing up a storm. He seems taken aback and starts trying to apologize. I cut him off and storm off, shaking with rage, impatience, and a flood of emotions. This is something I noticed in myself over the next several months: irritability and impatience with people and situations that I thought were wasting my time with petty concerns that were inconsequential. I normally wouldn't blow up at someone just asking for some change.

I board my train, which fills up and I stand and stare blankly out of the window. It seems like everyone is looking at me. It's crowded; everyone's going home. After a few stops I get a seat. I notice people still looking at me and one woman asks if I was "There". I said I was and she said, "I thought so. I didn't think you went to work like that." So I look at myself and, while I'm not that bad, I am disheveled and dirty, especially from the knees down from slogging through water and debris.

Before the Middletown stop the conductors make an announcement that medical and decontamination facilities have been set up at Middletown and anyone who was downtown should get off there. I get up and walk through a few cars until I find a conductor. I ask him what's going on and is there some reason I should get off; I'm thinking about what could have been on the planes again. He seems unconcerned and asks, "Do you feel alright?" I said yes and he says, "Then I don't see why you would get off unless it's your stop." I take his advice and walk back to get a seat where I meet a co-worker who worked on the 62nd floor. He shakes his head and smiles slightly as if in an expression of disbelief and relief. We briefly relate the events of the day and our own circumstances. We talked about how the terrorists knew what they were doing this time as opposed to the World Trade Center bomb attack in 1993 – to cause a progressive collapse from the top rather than trying to knock it down from the basement. We were engineers, after all, and had to analyze something. We also wondered at what would certainly be a huge death toll and at the prospects of knowing many who died.

We arrived at my station, Little Silver, and as I got off, I noticed a young mother holding an infant and pacing back and forth, waiting or hoping for a husband's and father's return. After I got in my car and drove away she was still waiting, bouncing her child slightly.

As I drive home it seems like my head is humming and things are happening around me and I am in an alternate time frame where things happening around me are either more frenetic or more lethargic than they should be or than I am. I think it was the beginnings of a slow release of the tension of the day. Very slow. Carolin said that I was distracted and unfocused for months after. Once, after I hung up the phone, I put it in the fridge. I did catch myself sometimes staring off blankly in the middle of situations when I should have been paying attention to something or someone.

16

Finally Home

I finally get home around 6:00 p.m. and pull into the driveway. Carolin comes out of the front door and we hug and kiss in the front yard. I tell her not to touch me too much because I don't know what's on me and I want to shower off. Carolin's mom, Rose, is there and she comes out and gives me a hug and leaves, knowing we probably need time alone to decompress. I rinse off with the hose in the back yard, stripping down to my boxers, and then go inside and take a shower. I think this is when I really notice the irritation in my throat and lungs. I have a cough that will be with me for months. My voice would become so hoarse that it was difficult to speak so people could understand me.

Carolin had thoughtfully bought some beer and when I was dressed I grabbed one and nearly guzzled it. It was the first of many that evening. That evening also became something of a blur in my memory and not just because of the alcohol. My head was still humming and I felt disconnected.

So the TV is on but I try not to look at it. I don't think I can handle seeing the coverage or even want to see it. I'm on the phone a lot of the time, relating the events of the day and telling everyone I'm fine. At first I just relate the basic sequence of events but every time I tell the story my mind seems to relax a little and I remember more events and details.

So I was on the phone with my mom, sitting in our living room, when I glance at the TV and see for the first time a replay of the second plane exploding through the South Tower. I'm absolutely stunned by the utter violence of the scene. "Oh, shit" I exclaimed, and dropped the phone. I am completely shaken. I pick up the phone and don't say anything. Then I say, "Mom. I'm sorry. I've got to go. I, uh, can't..." Then I think Carolin took the phone and finished my conversation for me. I just sat there for a bit with my hands to my face, I think for the first time starting to realize how violent it was and how close I had been to it all.

The night of September 11, 2001, Carolin and I went to bed and fell asleep holding each other. I fell asleep pretty quickly and slept soundly; I was drunk and the stress of the day was releasing. I would not sleep that well for the next couple of months. I wouldn't necessarily have trouble getting to sleep, but I would wake up around two or three in the morning and would not be able to get back to sleep.

17

Afterwards

The morning of September 12, 2001, I awoke around six in a panic and sat bolt upright. The rumble of a commuter train, the one I took to work, triggered my startle reflex and a brief panic. The sound brought back the same feeling I had in the stairwell when the other tower had collapsed – one of wondering what the hell is that and is it going to hit me. I shook uncontrollably and cried.

I spent much of September 12 immersed in the coverage of Ground Zero and the investigation into the attacks. I also spent the day wondering how many people I knew were killed and afraid to try to contact people for fear they would not be there. I had the e-mail address of one co-worker and sent a message, hoping for the best. He called me and he was so hoarse I could hardly understand him. But that was because he was sick, not because of the dust and smoke of the 11th. He had been in the cafeteria on the 43rd floor when the plane hit and he escaped in plenty of time. He actually saw live TV coverage of the second plane hitting the other tower when he was in some office space on the way down. He told me he knew of several people who were all right and I told him about Marco because that was the only person I knew was all right. Later I talked to other people and learned that everyone I worked with directly was all right except the guy who was headed back up the stairs and who I thought we had convinced to turn around. I cursed his stupidity until I learned he was all right, too.

Carolin took the rest of the week off to stay with me. I remember drinking quite a bit and going to the beach and talking to people on the phone about what happened. The next week I started periodically going into the Port Authority Technical Center in Jersey City where we were to set up temporary offices. I didn't really do anything. I just saw people who I had thought I would never see again and talked with people. The first normal, kind of social thing I did was to go to a Virginia Tech football game at Rutgers with Carolin a couple of weeks later.

At the end of September I started going to work more regularly in Jersey City. I shared an office with four people and two phones. The first week of October I went to the World Trade Center site with Port Authority personnel who were monitoring the dewatering operation at the site. I had free reign to walk around the site so I did. It was disorienting without the towers and with the devastation all around the site; it really seemed alien and not a place I had gone to work for five years. The recovery and cleanup operation seemed to be a loosely controlled chaos. Heavy machinery and people, including myself, were moving around everywhere without the usual controls you expect to see at normal construction sites. I thought there was no question that people would get hurt during the operation. I looked at where I had been and where I had run from the collapse, and it began to sink in even more just how close I had been to it all and to my demise. It was somewhat cathartic to return and see the devastation I had run from and not have to run away again.

Later in October I was at Newark Airport for work. I was on the telephone in Port Authority offices there talking to my boss. An airplane was taking off. The office I was in was near one of the runways. The roar grew in volume and I waited for it to start fading but it built to a point where I almost threw the phone down and ran out of the building in a panic attack. I was sure the plane was going to crash into the building. And the sound was very similar to the sound in the stairwell during the collapse. I somehow finished my conversation and then went home.

Even a year later, certain sounds still made me uneasy, though to a much lesser extent. I also had a compulsion to check on planes flying overhead and track them for a short while. Just to make sure.

My story is one of many about that day. There were countless moments of people helping each other, in ways large and small, to survive the day. One constant in all of them was the astounding and selfless service of all the first responders that day - FDNY, PAPD, NYPD, EMTs, and please forgive me if I can't remember all who responded and saved lives.

Today I often walk along the 9/11 Memorial reflecting pools at the WTC. I read the names engraved there of those who perished that day. I mourn their loss but also know there would have been many more names there without people helping each other that day and the actions of first responders and emergency workers. And I think about the firefighters I saw going up the stairs as I descended. And I think about the group of firefighters who showed us the way down when we were trapped on the 10th floor. And I think about the firefighters and police in the lobby who showed us the way out of the building. And I bow my head.

About The Authors

Bruce Walch, a graduate of Virginia Tech, is a civil engineer and works for the Port Authority of NY & NJ as an Environmental Engineer. From 1997 until September 1, 2001 his office was in 1 WTC. After the WTC was rebuilt, his office is now again at the World Trade Center. He and his wife Carolin (contributing author) love to travel around the world exploring new places and cultures.

Author Acknowledgments

Thank you to all of the family and friends who provided their love and support on 9/11 and in the aftermath of that day.

And to sister Mary Arczynski McGee and brother Dan Arczynski for their time spent reading the draft of this memoir and providing input and advice. And also to brother John Arczynski for his input.